30 Minutes ...To Get Promoted

DIANA CAMBRIDGE

KOGAN PAGE

First Indian Edition 2003
Reprinted 2008

Kogan Page India Private Limited
4737/23 Ansari Road,
Daryaganj
New Delhi 110 002

ISBN-10: 81-7554-216-0
ISBN-13: 978-81-7554-216-7

Published by Vinod Vasishtha for Kogan Page India Private Limited, 4737/23 Ansari Road, Daryaganj, New Delhi - 110 002.

Printed and bound at Print Perfect, New Delhi - 110 064.

CONTENTS

The 30 Minutes Series

The Kogan Page 30 Minutes Series has been devised to give your confidence a boost when faced with tackling a new skill or challenge for the first time.

So the next time you're thrown in at the deep end and want to bring your skills up to scratch or pep up your career prospects, turn to the *30 Minutes Series* for help!

Titles available are:
30 Minutes Before A Meeting
30 Minutes Before A Presentation
30 Minutes to Boost Your Communication Skills
30 Minutes to Boost Your Self Esteem
30 Minutes to Brainstorm Great Ideas
30 Minutes to Deal With Difficult People
30 Minutes to Get Your Own Way
30 Minutes to Get Promoted
30 Minutes to Improve Your Networking Skills
30 Minutes to Make the Right Decision
30 Minutes to Manage Your Time Better
30 Minutes to Market Yourself
30 Minutes to Master the Internet
30 Minutes to Motivate Your Staff
30 Minutes to Negotiate a Better Deal
30 Minutes to Plan a Project
30 Minutes to Solve that Problem
30 Minutes to Succeed in Business Writing
30 Minutes to Write a Business Plan
30 Minutes to Write a Marketing Plan
30 Minutes to Write a Report
30 Minutes to Write Sales Letters

Available from all good bookseller.
For further information on the series, please contact:

Kogan Page India Private Limited
2/13, Ansari Road, Daryaganj, New Delhi-110 002
Tel. 23258325, 23279280, 23283121, 23285874, Fax 0091 11 23267224

INTRODUCTION

We spend most of our lives working but put a small percentage of our effort into actively engineering our promotion. We tend to think of promotion as luck or fate or something that happens to other, more talented people. In fact there are techniques and tricks of the trade you can follow to climb up the management ladder.

You can get yourself selected for advancement (and earn more money) by taking on more responsibility and making a commitment to your immediate boss. Spending, say, half an hour a day doing extra things for your line manager will accelerate your promotion chances. One extra half day every six weeks doing your admin, and thinking up small cost-cutting and efficiency plans and ideas for new business will be a great asset to you.

Consider these two examples: a shoe shop assistant had the idea of colour-coding shoe boxes with tiny stars so that assistants could immediately pick out the right sizes. A junior manager in a DIY firm offered to build the company's Web site. Both ideas speeded up work, helped customers and staff, increased sales and were cheap to carry out. Within a year both employees had been promoted.

Turn every setback into success for you with your secret promotion plan. In Mrs Thatcher's famous words, bring solutions not problems to your place of work! By making the most of your energy and perseverance your chances of moving up and earning more money are enhanced 100 per cent.

Promotion isn't necessarily based on talent, but more on your approach to work, and your staying power. There are talented employees who become disenchanted, bored or feel they're under-valued. They get irritable and 'difficult'. Some start to take days off. If you put your energy into your 'promotion plan' even when you feel tired or bored, you'll definitely be rewarded.

You can begin your promotion plan at any time. Why not start today?

1

THINK SUCCESS

If you want promotion, begin your strategy today. Promotion begins not with qualifications on paper, but with what's in your mind. Commitment to yourself, your career plan and to your immediate boss is essential. Make yourself indispensable to your boss – take work off his or her hands, do it well and do it quietly.

You need to develop a strong work ethic, but the good news is you don't have to work day and night. Just working an extra half an hour every day on projects for your immediate boss will enhance your promotion prospects. Even if you have already been promoted, you can't count on further promotion being automatic: you still need to work at it. It's essential to keep up the momentum, even if at times you feel like quitting.

Written goals are always more effective than goals stored in your mind. You need to begin by putting your current goals in writing, maybe in a special notebook. Write down: your career goal for the next five years, your goal for the next six months and two small projects that you can plan and implement in the next three months. These goals and projects might be ideas for encouraging more customers to open accounts, or a simple plan for making things easier to find in the stock room. Perhaps you have ideas about cutting costs in your department, or about a team-building strategy you could manage, or you want to create a Web site for your company. Write these projects and goals down and you will have the key part of your career plan.

> **TIP**
>
> Don't worry if you haven't got a degree, an MBA or whatever. What counts towards promotion is how you perform at work.
>
> No one gets promoted with a nine-to-five mentality. You have to do more. Keep setting goals.

These are the five essential qualities that bosses look for in people they promote:

- reliability – always meeting deadlines and having a good attendance record;
- trustworthiness;
- willingness to accept responsibility;
- productivity;
- cheerfulness.

To this list you can add integrity – bosses need to count on their staff not passing on company secrets, dabbling in insider share dealing or risking the company's reputation by being drunk or taking drugs at work.

There are other important qualities you need to develop for your promotion kitbag:

- always be courteous;
- smile often;
- look smart;
- pass on helpful tips to colleagues;
- don't sulk or bear grudges;
- answer the phone with a welcoming voice.

Media bosses on a recruitment course defined their best daily newspaper editors as well groomed, ever-courteous, with a 'radiant' welcoming smile at all times. The men and women they singled out for promotion worked long hours when necessary, always had time for other staff members, were sociable and showed a sense of humour. Though most had an editorial background, they were also aware of the total picture – not just within their own newspapers, but the entire newspaper group. They took personal responsibility for learning all they could about budget control, advertising, sales and managing people.

A charming manner and good appearance are things you can cultivate and work at – you don't have to be born with them. In today's business arena, social skills are as crucial as vocational skills. Someone whose ideal job is one where he or she hides away most of the time (and that used to include many bosses) is unlikely to be suitable for promotion. You need to be interested in the entire company, not just your bit of it, and that means teaching yourself as well as going on courses. You teach yourself by networking to become more informed and spending time with colleagues from different departments.

Warning: try to never lose control in the office. For men this means not losing your temper and swearing at someone, for women it means not crying. If you ever feel upset and out of control (and everyone does sometimes) leave the office for ten minutes and walk about outside or have a coffee. You will be able to return feeling more poised.

> **TIP**
>
> Leaders reach people on an emotional level, as well as through their management skills.

Looking good for work

Doing well at work begins the moment you wake up! How organized is your morning routine? You can begin to 'think' your way into a new role using time management. Set your alarm for half an hour earlier than you need. Then you'll have time to pay attention to your appearance. Use uplifting bath oils and splash colognes to get you going.

Try to look reasonably good every day, rather than fantastic sometimes and a slob at others. Invest in haircuts and shoes – spend as much as you can afford on these two items and the rest of your outfit needn't be expensive. However, an expensive briefcase will always enhance your image.

Looking youthful is an asset, which can be annoying for older people. Short grey hair looks fine but men and women should avoid having straggling grey locks!

> **TIP**
>
> Women should always wear some make-up to work: they always look more confident and professional with a little make-up rather than barefaced.

Feeling good

First, don't skip breakfast. Eat or drink something early on that will energize you. Try *Get up and Go!* – a vitamin-packed powder breakfast drink you mix with juice (available by mail order from sales@highernature.co.uk).

Visualize yourself in your new role: spend five minutes every day just seeing yourself, strongly, as you'll be when you're promoted. Shut your eyes and focus on you, smiling, forceful and confident in your new role. The more you reinforce your vision of promotion, the more you're likely to succeed.

> **TIP**
>
> Hands and teeth are noticed at work — take care of yours.
>
> Wear deodorant at work – BO is offensive and would probably spoil your chances of promotion.

Fitting into the office culture

It's essential to fit into the office culture if you want to be promoted. Bosses look for people who:

- are clubbable;
- have a good network of contacts;
- show a sense of humour.

This means you do need to be able to socialize a bit. Don't be tempted to skip staff or floor meetings. If they're followed by a get-together in or out of the office, have at least one drink. If you feel shy, join a group near your manager. Lots of people avoid office socializing and tend to rush home. But if you want to get on, you do need to join in with the office culture. This includes bringing in cream cakes or standing a round of drinks when it's your birthday, having a night out twice a year with the people you work with or just attending the office bash at Christmas. It doesn't matter what it is – but you need to be there.

Communicating by e-mail

Put quality into all your office communication (including e-mail): make it courteous, prompt and helpful.

E-mail etiquette

When using e-mail:

- add the word 'thanks' to every request you make;
- don't write in capital letters;
- never be rude or sarcastic by e-mail;
- complete the conversation – send back a quick 'That's great, thanks' or 'Will do' or whatever's needed to complete the exchange;
- answer all e-mails within the day or as promptly as possible.

Begin to dress, behave and communicate the way a manager would – and start today.

Useful Web site for international seminars and private coaching on business goal-setting, health and fitness: **www.bright-idea.co.uk**

2

CHARACTER BUILDING

You already have the character traits that qualify you for promotion or you wouldn't be reading this book. But although the promotion path begins in the mind, those around you, especially your managers, are not mind-readers, so you have to demonstrate your ability.

Personal development

As you increase your personal power and strength, enhance your skills and stay focused, you will enjoy your own personal development. You will know you're moving towards your goal. One of the messages of this book is that life needn't be dull just because you intend to be promoted, but the discipline to persevere, to keep on reaching for goals despite setbacks, is a vital asset. Consider this example: a woman was promoted because she set herself the task of opening more customer accounts. All she did was ask every customer she served whether they'd like to open a credit account. Every assistant in the shop was asked to do the same, and they even got a small commission for each account opened. But the majority of sales assistants got fed-up after a few failures and abandoned card enquiries. The woman who kept going (who incidentally had left college with no qualifications) was noticed and promoted to 'motivator', encouraging co-workers to open more customer accounts. Within 18 months she was promoted to deputy floor manager.

Your behaviour while pursuing your goals is important. Don't complain; especially about things you could put right yourself. Be the one to fill up the photocopier with paper or untangle the fax machine. Be reliable: always meet deadlines. Don't get tangled up in office cliques.

Starting a romance

Try to keep your love life separate from your business life. Successful romances can begin at work, but starting them is risky. If the relationship goes wrong you'll feel very uncomfortable and you or the other person involved might even have to leave the company.

TIP

Three tips on keeping an office flirtation just that:

- Don't see the office party as a romantic arena – stay in a group, have fun, then leave early.
- Don't get involved in a steamy e-mail romance with a colleague.
- Do keep focused on your career aims.

Age is no barrier

If you're a mature employee – let's say over 45 years old – your age should not be a handicap to taking on increased responsibility and getting promoted, it should be an asset, so don't be ageist about yourself. Provided you have a cheerful, youthful, disciplined outlook, a sense of humour and can get on with younger colleagues, your maturity will not stand in your way at all.

The company could have 10 or 15 years of good work from you – probably more than from young people who tend to move jobs in the early years. Plus, you have both work and life experience and, if you were educated pre-1970s, your literacy skills may be far superior to those of youngsters. If you've brought up a family, you have practical skills and responsibility which young people may lack. But you do have to fit into today's workplace, which is much less formal, busier and more flexible than it was 20 years ago. Flexibility is the key word for your promotion prospects.

Dealing with the office environment

Try to put up with and adapt to any minor irritations in your office. If you find the office noisy, use earphones rather than complain; if it's too hot or too cold, dress accordingly. This can mean wearing summer clothes in winter, and vice versa at the office. Today's offices tend to be cramped and noisy, but one good thing about career progress is that as you move up, you often get more space!

TIP

A generally cheerful voice and manner is an asset. Use a sarcastic or ironic tone too often and people will be wary of you, and find you unapproachable (which is a disadvantage if you're aiming for promotion). It's good to see the funny side of work life and be able to lighten the atmosphere with a joke.

Coping with nerves

If you want to move up in the company, your voice needs to be heard. But you don't have to be a super-confident orator, or a chatterbox. Do speak up at meetings, making at least one contribution, even if you're basically shy. The more you do this, the less reserved you'll be.

If you're worried about how your voice sounds – maybe you think it sounds too quiet or too posh or too high – invest in some voice training. Ring a local dance and theatre school to see if they have voice projection classes. Look in *Yellow Pages* under Speech and Drama Tutors, many of them specialize in coaching businesspeople. You can also source acting lessons (through acting schools) for businesspeople.

Body language is important, but mainly to convey an impression of energy and alertness. Move around the office

TIP

Nervous before going into a meeting? Try clenching everything – buttocks, chest and jaw – before you step through the door. As you release, you'll feel instantly relaxed.

briskly and purposefully – no slouching or putting your head down on your desk.

Work at home

Willingness to do extra work at home is a characteristic of someone who will be promoted. Think of the work you do at home as a pleasure and not a chore. You can use the time to study reports in a more detailed way, draft ideas and letters and bone up on the training manual.

Home practicals

It's useful to have:

- A computer at home so that you can do some work in your spare time on floppy disks and send e-mails.
- A year planner with deadlines marked in red.
- Colourful ring binders in which you can keep memos, notes from your boss and your replies. Every time you get a piece of paper, a chart or memo you don't want to lose, add it to your file. This becomes your 'work-book' and you can easily take it home.
- Coloured 'Post-Its' at work and at home to remind you of items and phone numbers you might need.

TIP

Don't fall into the 'comfort trap' at work. If it becomes too easy and comfortable, you'll lose the incentive to move on up and after a while you'll become bored. Aim to be resourceful. If you keep taking opportunities your work life will always offer challenge.

Useful Web site: heading to 50 and seeking promotion? The *I Don't Feel Fifty* site at **www.idf50.co.uk/home.asp** has informative features for older people on topics ranging from health to work.

3

GO A BIT FURTHER

The person who gets promoted is the one who goes that bit further. Don't just wait to carry out instructions, but suggest ideas for improving the business, for getting new clients or changing the way something is done. Take all the training you can, including courses in your spare time. People chasing promotion do not make personal phone calls, gossip or chat when there's a lull in workload. Instead they do things that will move the company on. They're constantly busy and productive, turning out quality work.

If there's something you enjoy doing which you have a talent for, suggest in writing to your line manager that you take it on. It could be any of the following:

- doing some PR for your company;
- dealing with customer complaints;
- using your second language to increase business;
- coaching beginners in telephone skills;
- sorting out records that everyone else has found a reason not to tackle;

- arranging training courses;
- helping work-experience trainees to settle in.

Someone has to do all these jobs and, particularly in a small company, anyone willing to tackle them on top of their own work will be valued.

Keep learning

Maybe there's a part of your work that worries you – perhaps giving presentations or dealing with some aspect of new technology. It's a good idea to buy in your own training. If you choose a private coach the investment will be worth it for the increased confidence. Alternatively, look in *Yellow Pages* for your local further education college. Larger colleges offer a range of part-time business courses (including many dealing with information technology and with presentation skills).

If your own firm offers training, take advantage of it. Companies often find that they have spare places on some courses because employees find reasons to drop out more often than attend. So it's worth putting your name down for last-minute cancellations. If your company has training manuals, work steadily through them.

If there's something special you'd like to learn, ask your manager whether the firm will fund training. Don't be downcast if your request is refused, it just means that, like all companies, yours has to cut costs and may even have a freeze on outside training. Be resourceful – see if you can do a modified version of the training yourself, perhaps by buying a book and video on it.

One form of coaching you might like to consider is NLP (Neuro-Linguistic Programming). This is a well-respected business and sales tool and especially useful to help you with the perseverance and staying power you need for promotion.

NLP can help you to:

- think 'strong';
- turn negative thoughts into positive ones;
- set goals and reach them;
- develop instant rapport with others;
- be more persuasive;
- achieve excellence in work.

Be your own PA

Good word-processing skills are important for any top job. Today's bosses don't expect to have a team of secretaries and personal assistants. Many managers prepare all their own letters, reports and presentations: they may have a shared secretary but that job will mainly involve organization, not copy typing.

The more you can be your own PA, the more useful you will be to the firm. Knowing how to perform simple tasks like attaching a new mouse or cleaning an old one, or unblocking a jammed photocopier, for example, are all extremely useful.

TIP

Learn how to do spreadsheets – if you want to be a manager this is a great asset.

Check, check and check your work again. Make proof-reading all your work second nature.

Employees with fast, excellent word-processing and computer skills are sought after as managers because they bring added value to the company.

It's worth learning about e-mail and the Internet, and how to write for the Web. You could be even more of an asset to your company if you acquire some desktop publishing skills (perhaps in Quark or Aldus Pagemaker). Many companies want to produce materials in house, such as publicity newsletters, magazines, shoppers' lists, or press releases.

Sales success

> **TIP**
>
> Aim to have a mix of both creative and commercial skills.
>
> Could you build a Web site? If you could, and you work in a small company and seek promotion, offer this.

As more and more retailers combine, opportunities in customer sales are increasing: retailers are constantly looking for employees willing and able to both manage other people and sell goods. In shops, if you're able to go that bit further, to supervise and sell, your career will flourish. Look towards this dual role for promotion.

Seven career tips for super sales assistants:

1. Offer ideas to increase sales.
2. Keep a vigilant eye on shop security (reducing shoplifting is a major part of some retail work).
3. Help colleagues with problems.
4. Coach new staff in selling and in using the tills.
5. Stay late without complaint.
6. Smile at every customer.
7. Think of new ways of keeping the stockroom tidy.

If you work in a small shop, and have started as a junior sales assistant, simply by following these seven tips to seize more and more responsibility you could be shop manager within a couple of years. If you already manage a small shop, take an interest in the wider picture: ask if you can visit other branches, attend conferences or receive copies of appropriate reports.

> **TIP**
>
> If you work in a shop, keep thinking of 'add-ons' your shop could offer. What would customers who use your services also be interested in?

Play the game

If you have to take part in business games or role-playing try to join in cheerfully even if you don't enjoy it. After all, it's just a few hours out of your life. Many companies now value 'fulfil your own potential' workshops – and fulfilling your own potential may mean punching a piece of wood, standing on a chair or doing something that seems equally daft. Unfortunately you will have to grit your teeth and bear it. If you're honest, announce that the whole thing seems a waste of time and you're not going to do it, your chances of promotion will rapidly decrease.

> **TIP**
>
> Aim to be stoic and get through something you dislike, such as a course where you have to make a fool of yourself or join in a silly game. Refuseniks dig their own career graves!

Stay the course

Staying power is vital if you want promotion. It's more important than talent. Many of us begin a new job well and can be earmarked as achievers. Yet when the adrenaline of the new job wears off and a few difficulties, or difficult people, have to be tackled, that first sparkle can wane.

You can mark yourself out as promotion-worthy just by keeping up the enthusiasm despite any setbacks. Try to be at your 'interview best' as often as you can. The more you can keep this up, the easier it gets. Being able to react positively is a learned skill, and gets easier with practice.

TIP

Keep acting as if you have that desired promotion. It won't be instant, but the pay-off will come.

Work on your staying power as well as than your 'first impression' persona. Don't beat yourself up emotionally if you do have 'off days' – just don't have too many!

Useful Web site for more information on NLP courses: **www.nlp-community.com**

4

YOU AND YOUR BOSS

You'll go a long way with your boss if you make a personal, private commitment to putting his or her work first. Commit strongly and respond well again and again to requests that other workers grumble about. Be the one who never has to be e-mailed a second time or reminded about reports, admin or sales charts.

Always give priority to whatever your boss asks and try to turn it around in 24 hours, even if it means working late. An extra half an hour spent daily on just your boss's requests will reward you well. Most people will leave stuff from the boss to the last minute, resenting it all the way. Try to get work to your manager well ahead of time – be the first in with it!

Open all you boss's e-mails first and respond to them promptly. Make your replies brief. When things in the office are stressful, a touch of humour is often appreciated. Try not to knock on your manager's door to ask for advice or meetings. Think in terms of saving his or her time. Verbal communication takes up time, so instead of communicating ideas, suggestions or responses verbally, put things in writing.

Always deliver what you say you'll deliver, but do not expect 'stroking' for work done quickly and well. Bosses value highly employees who consistently meet high targets but who don't crave applause. The payback will come later. The responsibility for maintaining a good relationship with you boss lies with you, not with him or her.

TIP

Never use the word 'try' to your boss, as in 'I'll try to have that report in by tomorrow at five o'clock'. Your reply is always 'I'll have it ready by five o'clock tomorrow'.

Welcome routine chores

Be on top of your admin. If you hate doing forms, accounts or timesheets and are often late with them, schedule in one morning every six weeks when you can concentrate on them in 'out of work' hours. At first it will seem tedious, but you'll be surprised how productive you can be when you concentrate on just admin. Often admin seems boring – well, it often is boring – but your boss has the even worse job of collating it. Chasing up consistent late-comers is an extra burden for a manager. No matter how good you are at the creative side of work, low-grade admin gives you a black mark. Think of each bit of boring admin successfully completed as another step towards that promotion.

> **TIP**
>
> Always make your boss look good. If group hostility seems to be directed at him or her, say something to lighten the atmosphere or offer your boss support. Don't be afraid of being singled out by colleagues as the boss's pet. Colleagues won't promote you; your boss will!

Develop your relationship with your boss

Chemistry between you and your boss is important. But this is created over time, not overnight. So don't worry if things are not immediately easy between you. By your solid hard work and loyalty you'll create a rapport. You can improve the rapport by 'mirroring': if your boss tends to speak slowly and carefully, adopt a similar style; if he or she is a fast talker with a strong sense of humor,

> **TIP**
>
> Companies don't promote 'yes-men' – it's a short-term gain. So although a junior manager may appear to always agree with the boss, you can bet that in private they have disagreements, with the junior manager finding fault (politely) in the top manager's plan. By now they will know each other quite well. Bosses want managers who are strong, not weak.
>
> Never gossip to colleagues about your boss.
>
> Never pass on information your boss gives you.

reflect that. If your boss reacts to problems with a joke rather than agonizing, adopt this light-hearted response up to a point but remember he or she is still taking it very seriously. If you have a more earnest boss who tends not to make many jokes, follow that example. Mirroring is a question of tact and common sense – you can still be yourself.

If your boss asks you to lunch or for a drink, that's a good sign. But always remember you're still at work: even if your boss is around your age and similar to you in style, don't imagine he or she is going to be your best friend. If your boss talks about personal matters such as holidays, family or home, respond with interest. One thing your boss will never do – or shouldn't do – is criticize his or her own boss to you, so that's something you never think of doing.

Let your manager introduce work topics, and follow the lead. Think of it as a 'working lunch' or 'working drink' rather than a social occasion. Be enthusiastic and optimistic about work topics, welcoming any change he or she suggests. At the end of each social encounter your boss will think of you as a positive and helpful person, an asset to the company. But don't ask 'How am I doing?' or 'Am I doing OK?' over a drink or snack – keep that kind of feedback for your appraisal.

Your boss will value your view 'from the floor'. Never gossip about or rubbish fellow workers. But you can relay to him the 'mood' of your department or details of any procedures that seem to need changing. Be honest and unemotional here as the boss may get enough resentment and whingeing from other workers. Always be positive, for example: 'I think it will take people a little while to get used to the new Internet ordering system, but it could work very well.'

Your boss may seem friendly – remember he or she has been promoted partly because of social skills – but he or she won't become a close friend now because a boss's commitment is to the company and the career it offers, not to individuals within it. Aim to be your boss's helpful aide: someone to be trusted and relied upon. This is the role your boss plays to his or her boss.

TIP

At a lunch or drinks session, your boss is the main player. Don't try to set the agenda. Let your boss introduce topics, invite comments, set the tone – and pay the bill! You should offer politely to pay your way, but he or she won't let you. Never insist on paying for yourself.

Useful Web site for advice on better working relationships: **www.qsilvertlc.com**

5

WORKING WITH OTHERS

Aiming for promotion does not mean being a toady. Employers look for team players who gain respect from colleagues, have persuasive skills and can see ideas from different points of view. Managers promote people with the strength of character to tell them, politely and in private, that their idea for selling electric blankets in Saudi Arabia is crazy – and suggesting one or two more promising ideas.

Once a decision has been taken, however, managers want you to support it when they sell it to the staff. People resist change and come up with many reasons for disliking a new idea. You need the courage to be the one who says it's worth a try or that though it may seem cumbersome at first, it will be more efficient in the long run. Expect your promotion chances to be weakened if you join in with the general 'We don't want it' response to change. You have to be flexible and prepared to welcome change now.

Difficult people

Often doing well at work isn't just a matter of the actual work, but of dealing with the people you work with. If only they were all the same as you. But they're not, and some of them will definitely be difficult. Difficult people are always there and working with someone you dislike is unavoidable. If we all refused to work with people we didn't like, most of the businesses in the country would come to a standstill.

How will you cope with a prickly or unco-operative colleague? It may be that this person isn't really dreadful but just different in personality to you. He or she may be more assertive, extrovert, even a touch aggressive. You have to get on with him or her if you're to get things done. This person is unlikely to change, so if you want promotion, accept the responsibility for making this tricky relationship work.

You need to accept that it isn't necessary to like everyone at work, or for them to like you. Fit in with nuisance people, so that they have no complaints about your work. Don't try to become friends or seek out these people's company, all that's needed is that you 'rub along' at work. Be pleasant and neutral even when they are a pain: don't try to get them to like you.

Four tips for dealing with awkward people:

- don't respond to annoying remarks;
- don't get involved in their petty disputes;
- don't make an official complaint;
- remember it won't just be you who finds someone troublesome – difficult people are generally unpopular.

> **TIP**
>
> Never waste time worrying about what people are saying about you – there's nothing you can do about it. It really doesn't matter. The higher up you go, the more people will talk about you. And it still doesn't matter! If you want promotion, think strong and develop a thicker skin.

Chat attacks

Another problem can be working with someone you like! If you find that chatting and laughing with a colleague you like distracts you from work, you may need to do something about it. Your friend may not be as promotion-hungry as you are – so what do you do? You don't want to spoil the friendship, but you do want to focus on your work. Again you'll have to take the responsibility for keeping the friendship manageable. Try to move the friendship to the after-hours part of your life, keeping office time free to promote your career.

When your friend starts chatting on Monday morning, say 'Yes, I've got loads to tell you. Shall we have a drink after work tomorrow?'. Arrange to have lunch together once a week, or do a course or go to the gym together so you have a regular date.

Perhaps you sit near your friend. Try moving your seat away slightly so you aren't quite so vulnerable to chat attacks. But make the move seem natural. Don't upset your friend – people you really get on with are essential allies.

> **TIP**
>
> If you have children, don't go on about them in the office. Workers who do this are seen as less ambitious and less motivated.

Be a tactful teacher

You may have to check other people's work in your job. The better you are at coaching and supervising, the more you enhance your promotion prospects. If someone has done a job that still needs some revision, tactful ways of asking for amendments are:

'It's fine – it just needs a few tweaks here and there.'

'I've had a look at it and it looks great. But we need a bit more detail on these few points...'

Always thank other people for the work they've done. Always give tips and advice that will help them amend the work and advance their skills.

> **TIP**
>
> Bosses look for people who can coach and check without being resented. Aim to be relaxed, courteous and helpful, and learn to see yourself as coaching rather than correcting.
>
> People who can 'finish' (check details, chase deadlines and ensure the process is completed) are sought after by bosses. But the nature of the task can mean being unpopular in the office. Don't let this put you off.

TIP

Treat all situations and people with integrity. Don't be nicer to people you like – or at least not in the office!

Be fair. In a small meeting, it shouldn't be only your voice which is heard, other people should also speak.

Listen – don't talk

Listening skills are very valuable and you can acquire them. The best managers are always great listeners. They let you speak while they listen carefully. You'll often find in a one-to-one situation these managers don't say much at all, but just by listening to you they make you feel better, valued, understood. The trick they have learnt is to let the other person talk, so use this trick yourself with co-workers. Don't interrupt or rush in with advice.

Seven ways to get on better with co-workers:

- handle people's feelings carefully;
- share a drink now and then with colleagues;
- be kind if someone feels unwell: see if they can go early;
- don't ring colleagues at home to ask why they're away;
- make coffee for fellow workers;
- coach – if someone's struggling with a task, help them;
- never make fun of people for not understanding something.

Support others

Colleagues are sometimes surprisingly poor at supporting each other in times of trouble. 'I just didn't know what to say' is a common reaction to someone else's bad fortune. If a colleague is made redundant, or suffers serious illness, for example, put something in writing to them. A brief note or card saying you're sorry it should happen to them is always appreciated.

If someone asks you for a reference or for advice on their own career, respond promptly. Try to respond to these requests in 24 hours as they're very important to people. If you can do this, you'll get pay-off later. When you are promoted, you'll find you already have a platform of loyalty.

TIP

Be generous. Remember colleagues' birthdays, contribute to office collections without complaint and buy your team a drink, an ice cream or surprise sweets now and then. Good bosses are usually generous people and people who are personally mean don't make good managers. When it comes to company cash though, the meaner the better!

Useful Web site: simple yoga stretches you can do at your desk on a bad day from **www.will-harris.com/yoga**.

6

WHEN SETBACKS STRIKE

No matter how careful and conscientious you are, mistakes happen. The man or woman who hasn't made a mistake hasn't made anything. Be prepared to own up to your mistakes. To err is human; to deny responsibility for mistakes is foolish. People who think they're infallible are menaces, no matter how talented they might be. Rigid, blinkered attitudes are not assets in today's workplace; they're liabilities. Bosses tend not to promote people who aren't big enough to own up gracefully. If an error of yours is uncovered, accept responsibility. Say something like:

> 'I'm sorry I miscalculated the figures. It was my mistake, but I can produce a new report if I work late tonight and tomorrow, so I'll do that.'

> 'I managed to lose the report summary, or most of it – my fault not the computer's. I've still got the notes so I'll redo it all this evening.'

Never blame anyone else.

> **TIP**
>
> Never ask if you should redo faulty work. Always take it for granted that you will correct it.

When requests are refused

If your request for something such as a new project, extra resources or training is turned down, accept it philosophically. Keep coming up with new ideas even if some are rejected. A good strategy is to send a brief note, perhaps by e-mail, within 24 hours of a rejection along the lines of: 'Thanks for looking at my idea. I can see it does need more work on it. I'll take up your suggestions and get back to you with fresh ideas – thanks again. David.' In your note, refer to a comment made in the rejection so that it's clear you understand your boss's point of view.

An idea that isn't taken up will not do your career any harm – quite the opposite. The vast majority of employees never offer a single idea for improving their own company. So workers who are 'alive' in this way are very much valued. Keep those ideas coming!

Difficult situations

If the company has to make staff cuts, share the increased workload willingly. There's always a drop in morale after redundancies. Try to keep people's spirits up rather than joining in with the general gloominess. If it was your boss who had to tell people they were being made redundant, he or she has faced a grim task. If you quietly acknowledge this, your comment will go down well.

> **TIP**
>
> When you plan projects build in some setback time to allow for the unexpected. If you don't have to use it, you'll get your project in ahead of time. If you do have to use it, you'll still be on time.

Stay on track

Stamina is probably the number one strength in your promotion kitbag. You need to be able to focus on promotion and tackle your job well, day in, day out. That means you may need to re-energize yourself at work from time to time. Everyone has those headachy 'can't go on' afternoons now and then. Recognize the feeling?

You can beat a bad hour if you:

- tidy something – a drawer, your desktop, a display unit;
- add new names and contacts to a database;
- buy sweets or nuts to share round;
- e-mail a 'positive' friend for a one-line chat.

This is your worst-case scenario: you thought promotion was just round the corner, but someone else gets it this

> **TIP**
>
> One way to perk up a more prolonged 'doldrums' time is by buying something new to wear at work. This need not be a major purchase, it could be some budget jewellery, a new shirt, a tie, winter gloves and scarf, or new cologne. You'll freshen up your self-image and give yourself more vitality.

time. This is a real setback. Keep smiling! Congratulate the lucky man or woman. Send them a nice note or e-mail. Save your four-letter words for when you get home. Then keep working through your promotion plan as before. Most likely you were just a bit premature – you need to work on getting promoted for a bit longer. Above all, don't get resentful or grumpy. The next promotion could be yours.

> **TIP**
>
> If you're going through a bad time, take up a comforting project to look forward to after work. This could be anything from a small home improvement to cooking a special meal or doing a short easy course.

Are you in 'downtime' this minute? You need superquick fixes if you're to get back on the promotion track! Today you could:

- buy yourself a new paperback by your favourite author: or an inspiring how-to book (try anything by personal power guru Anthony Robbins or mind, body and spirit visionary Leslie Kenton);
- treat yourself to two new magazines on a topic that will please you;
- book up an aromatherapy session soon. Rose geranium is a good oil for stress and depression.
- arrange to play badminton, go paintballing or horse-riding – something you're good at or have always wanted to try.

Think 'strong'

One of the least helpful things to do in a down phase is to get together with a workmate who's also fed-up. You end up having a moaning session and maybe making plans to leave (which could scupper your promotion strategy).

Another unhelpful thing is to go home in the evening and sit staring at the wall. You need to fill your mind with something other than your depression, such as a book, a film, a meal, and perhaps a glass of wine!

Never tell your boss you feel hard done by, or complain that you've been treated unfairly. He or she will just remind you that life isn't fair.

TIP

It's OK to feel down at work. Everyone does. But try not to talk about it. Pretend you're an actor playing a happy worker – smile and chat. Oddly, this seems to work and before long you'll feel better.

Barriers to promotion can come from you. By thinking in a negative way you sabotage your own efforts. Instead of thinking 'This is awful. I can't stand it. I'll never be promoted now' think 'I feel a bit down today. But I've been feeling good here, and I expect to feel good again soon. I expect to be promoted.' (Think 'strong').

Useful Web site for staying calm at work during setbacks: **www.calmcentre.com**

7

TAKE RESPONSIBILITY

Don't just accept responsibility, grasp it. Be the one to deal with a problem, even if it's not a problem that comes strictly within your remit. You can be the one to sort out even small problems, like the cleaning lady not being able to find the bin bags, or a colleague having left her pass-key at home. Get a reputation for being helpful.

A college leaver who joined a contract publishing company as a receptionist often stayed late just to watch the magazines being completed. Since most procedures were done on desktop, she began to pick up the editorial and production stages. She also sussed out which tasks the editorial staff found a nuisance – phone calls chasing copy, fact-checking calls, sending out voucher magazines, faxing text – and she offered to take on some of these, dealing with them when reception was quiet.

Just by observing and copying the editors, she was able to learn a lot – but that alone wouldn't have been enough for promotion. She also chose to shoulder more responsibility. Within a year she had been promoted to editorial assistant, and within three years she was a deputy editor. Five ways to layer **more responsibility** into your job:

- add **more detail** when writing reports – go a bit further;
- **forward plan** your tasks for three months ahead, in writing;
- **coach** a colleague who's finding a system difficult;
- offer to be a **mentor** (if you have experience in company systems and are more mature, you can advise and steer someone younger in their career);
- understand how to manage a **budget.**

Now here are things it's *not* worth taking responsibility for if you want to be promoted. That's not to say these aren't worthwhile but they won't help you to a better job. They might use up your energy on trivia. They are:

- the office noticeboard;
- the first-aid box;
- the stationery cupboard.

Problem-solving

Taking responsibility for solving problems is a key part of being a manager. Observe how managers you admire do it, and learn to copy them. They may tackle an obstacle with:

- a **sense of humour** – making people laugh so they forget their grievances;
- a **non-judgemental attitude** – dealing with the problem without assigning blame;
- a **positive** approach – not wallowing in problems but moving swiftly to solutions.

Basically, the excellent manager is a problem-solver and a team player, who acknowledges everyone and treats everyone in the same fair and courteous manner. Such managers show a responsible attitude to others' welfare.

Communicate with more people

Good managers don't hide away in their offices, they're 'visible'. If you're not a natural extrovert, you'll have to make an effort to be more visible. The more you do it, the easier it gets! Try being on cheerful 'having a word' terms with everyone in the office, from receptionist to office cleaner, rather than just chatting to your immediate team. Yes, it does need effort – it's so much easier to come in, sit down and chat only to your team, but that's how most of us can get into a rut.

You'll probably have to go out of your way to have a word with newcomers and people you don't work directly with, but it's worth it. 'How are you?' or 'How's it going?' said with a smile is enough to start you off. Get into the habit of having this brief word with most people, so you get to know more or less everyone in your department or building.

TIP

Listen when people tell you things: try not to 'top' their awful experience with one of yours.

Be a good host

If you're at a work meeting, lunch or reception and feeling slightly exposed, take on a little responsibility (and feel more comfortable at the same time) by:

- offering others food and drinks – playing 'host' rather than guest;
- looking out for company newcomers, and chatting to them;
- showing visitors around;
- offering to do any chauffeuring needed;
- giving out company material, or getting people to sign in;
- volunteering to research something;
- offering to co-ordinate a small committee or project;
- if your guests are from out-of-town, suggesting local beauty spots, sites of historic interest or restaurants they could visit.

When you have a definite role to play, you feel much less reticent. So expanding the scope of what you do will actually increase your confidence. Plus, your helpful attitude can't but be noticed and approved – unlike the rest of the staff you haven't just headed for the drinks tray and chatted to your mates!

What not to do

Warning: taking on more responsibility doesn't mean being bossy, or giving the impression you know better. No matter how brilliant show-offs are at their jobs, employers are wary of them. It's essential that others find you easy and pleasant to work with. Being quietly calm and steady (but not timid) isn't a handicap to promotion.

Seven ways to *dent* career chances:

- boast about how good you are at something;
- try to do too much, too fast, too stressfully;

- criticize the way other people do things;
- make fun of anyone – be very discreet instead;
- gossip – if you don't join in you'll gain respect;
- lose your temper;
- display prejudice – against people who are old, overweight, gay, from a different culture and so on.

Read it up

It's useful for managers-to-be to have a basic working knowledge of the following three things:

- company law – especially aspects of employment law like hiring and firing, disciplinary procedures, statutory benefits;
- unions and how they work;
- your own company history – ask your HR department for any leaflets.

(You can buy inexpensive how-to books on all aspects of business: try the **Amazon** on-line store for a huge range).

Begin to read a quality newspaper every day – a different one each day if you like. Watch TV documentaries about top business gurus or business advisors giving information to flagging businesses. These programmes are entertaining and easy to watch and through them you'll pick up good nuggets of sound business advice. The more informed you are the better your career prospects.

> Useful Web site for books on business, creativity and motivation from *Creativity Unleashed* at **www.cul.co.uk/books**

8

CHALLENGE FOR SUCCESS

Challenge embedded notions at work. If something's been done in a certain way for 50 years but doesn't seem to be working well now, try to think of a better way to do it. But remember – don't try to fix things that aren't broken. Bosses like people with common sense who approach change with an open mind.

Someone who tells you firmly 'We've always done it this way and that's the way I'm going to do it' is unlikely to ever be a boss. Yes, there are some traditions worth preserving. One example of this is 'the customer is always right', but ways of dealing with customers have changed. The successful company is changing and evolving all the time. For example, one thing you might challenge is the idea of 'scripted' responses to customers. Ask if you could have a trial run with unscripted responses, and see how many new or repeat orders you can achieve.

Another new trend is encouraging workers to shop on-line from work – making it easier for them to work longer hours. It's essential when offering new ideas either to ask for a trial run, carry one out if you can, or offer some evidence that your idea could work.

Get it right

When you're thinking about ideas or plans for the company, get things right more times than you get them wrong. Don't guess at sales figures or the customer complaints ratio – this sort of information will be available somewhere within the company. HR staff can be your first port of call. They should be able to advise you on where to access factual information. When you're putting ideas in writing, only use hard facts as your background.

Be bold – write proposals or outlines for projects you know you could take on. Don't worry that you'll come over as arrogant or a show-off. Employees who show they want to seize opportunities and can put their ideas in writing delight bosses. If you know you have a good idea, you can almost write your own job description. But remember – don't ask for any money yet! Just outline what you might do, the *benefits* to the company, and the cost (although preferably no cost should be involved).

TIP

Show initiative. Can you think of a way for the company to do something faster? Put it in writing to your boss.

Find mentors

Most people just do their job and go home. But you're career-conscious and you want to get on. You can do your job in a different, more challenging way from your colleagues – maybe by finding a mentor (or being one), trying a bit of networking and deliberately expanding the scope of how you operate.

Can you identify mentors or people who will help you at work? A mentor is a kind of career patron, but in reality this could mean anyone useful and helpful in developing your career. It could be anyone from Tony G in Sales or Mary B in PR to someone in a different company, or in a business club.

The mentors you should consider will have the kind of jobs you aspire to (they'll probably be working at one stage up from you). You'll have met them at a company or industry event and seen they're friendly, approachable and on the same wavelength as you. They will be clearly as keen on work as you are. Don't even try to connect with anyone who seems frosty or very preoccupied – there'll be enough friendly helpful types to approach.

In a large modern company workers are encouraged to share knowledge and be helpful to one another, so e-mail a possible mentor or ask them for 15 minutes of their time. Don't feel shy about this as people love being asked for their advice. Then you can find out the practicalities of the job you're aiming for, such as how they arrange their day, how much time is spent on figures and budgeting, or how many meetings they attend or hold.

Just ask

Ask your mentor about:

- books and magazines they recommend;

- business clubs worth joining;
- useful Web sites;
- when they first got promoted;
- which training courses are most useful;
- the part of their job they find hardest;
- three main qualities important for their role.

Write a few notes afterwards to remind yourself what they've said. Thank your mentor by note or e-mail, and keep in touch for extra advice – they'll enjoy the ego boost of being a sort of career guru!

> **TIP**
>
> Keep your mentoring plans to yourself! Only promotion-hungry workmates are likely to understand. You don't have to justify your career agenda to anyone.
>
> Diversify. Let's say you're a credit controller or a junior systems manager – that doesn't mean you can't learn about sales or marketing or PR. Pick up as much as you can about whatever you're interested in, from business books and contacts within the company. There's nothing to stop you.

Network now

Construct your own network of contacts, and cultivate them. Networking means creating a business friendship, but without the usual slowish friendship development. You can go straight to asking a favour (advice or information on work) from your network contacts. Always send a note or e-mail of thanks promptly. When you meet someone at a seminar or presentation, you'll find you can get to know him or her quite quickly within a day. Follow up that first meeting with a note or e-mail – the person might be friendly enough to suggest a quick coffee, or you could. It's fine for you to make the first move.

At any company event (except the office party when everyone wants to forget work) you can network. You can network at:

- an in-house training session, seminar or conference;
- a conference attended by representatives of many different companies;
- a sales trip or exhibition;
- a reception hosted by your company.

It's essential to have business cards, so create your own from your computer if the company doesn't provide them. Names and e-mails scribbled on napkins and scraps of paper get lost and look scruffy. Hand out your cards generously: once someone has your card and you have his or hers it's very easy to make contact. For some reason, everyone enjoys being given business cards!

TIP

Put warmth into every exchange. Make your dealings with customers, colleagues, managers and network contacts as warm and friendly as possible. Good managers aren't cool and remote. Practise being warm and see how it rewards you.

As you make new career contacts, stay well organized: your contacts may visit you unexpectedly at your office! Make sure you:

- keep a neat desk and briefcase (and perhaps car);
- maintain an up-to-date contacts book;
- ask for business cards or create your own;
- don't have lots of toys, pictures and jokes around your computer.

TIP

Never take your promotion for granted. You have to earn it. And you will!

Useful Web site for being more informed: **www.newspapers.com** which gives a list of online newspapers across the world.

9

THE JOB'S YOURS!

Take on more and more, steadily and carefully, and wait for the right opportunity to ask for that promotion. It could be when a job vacancy higher up the management ladder is advertised internally, or at your next appraisal meeting.

Applying formally for promotion

Most firms advertise their vacancies internally, so watch the noticeboards and staff newsletters. Monitor the gossip. Word of a resignation or sacking usually gets around before the official memo. Keep an eye on the company's expansion or re-organization plans. There could be an opportunity for you. The more time you have to prepare your application the better.

The job advertisement will ask for written applications. There'll be no exceptions for internal candidates. A word to Joe in Personnel saying you'd like the job won't be good enough. But as a matter of policy companies normally interview internal candidates, so your written application need not be as detailed and comprehensive as if you were writing from the outside. The company will already have most of your CV on file, and they'll know a lot about you. You'll start with a big advantage.

Keep the application brief, but not dismissively so. Set out what you've achieved in your current post, with written evidence to back up your successes, and explain why your promotion would benefit the company. Say you look forward to the opportunity of discussing your application in greater detail should the company want to take it to the interview stage.

Don't assume that because you're an internal candidate the job is yours. There could be other colleagues who are just as promising and as ambitious as you. The company's preference for this post might be for fresh blood from outside.

Be convincing at the interview

Your role at the interview is to convince the interviewer that you can bring new ideas and enthusiasm to the job, plus the valuable detailed knowledge of the company that external candidates won't have. Go well prepared to the interview with a detailed but concise chronicle of your successes. Be confident. Have clear ideas about how you would tackle the new job, especially its problem areas, and some constructive comments about the company's general position and future. Put yourself in the interviewer's shoes, think about the questions you would ask and plan convincing answers. Look for the weaker spots in your own application and be prepared for tough questions on them. When you've done all this, you'll have done your best. All you can do now is wait for the decision.

Handling an appraisal

Approach your appraisal seriously. Remember that the manager doing the appraisal isn't at the head of the corporate food chain. Many managers don't like doing appraisals and are embarrassed by the whole business, especially appraising someone they work closely with every day. If you make it as easy as possible for the appraiser, that's another step up your promotion ladder. Prepare well for your appraisal. This includes going in with practical suggestions for training that would benefit you and the company.

Give credit

When you review your achievements, never claim the credit for other people's good ideas. Not only is this dishonest, but also you'll probably be found out. Not getting due credit is one of the reasons good people leave jobs and go elsewhere, so you could be responsible for this if you take credit for other's work. Instead, give credit where it's due and win brownie points for yourself for getting the best out of people and encouraging initiative. A manager's job is to motivate good people, not push them to the competition next door.

Don't react to criticism

Your appraisal might include some comments from your boss which sound like criticism, but don't spoil your good work by getting cross. Don't react emotionally. If you think the criticism is unfair, say so politely, giving reasons. The employee who is promotion material is not defensive or angry when criticized. You have to accept that not everyone will approve of you and it may be that jealous colleagues do want to push the knife in. Get used to it. Those knives will probably be even sharper when you're promoted!

Asking for more money

When the next pay review comes round, it's time to ask for a salary increase. At this stage be careful not to price yourself out of the market: your increase should reflect your extra work but still make it seem like a company saving. You, one person, are doing the work of another whole or half person but not costing the firm anything like one-and-a-half or two people. Outline in writing the ways in which you've helped the company – particularly in cost-cutting or generating new business – and ask for your salary to be increased, without necessarily putting a figure on it.

Remember:

- never ask for more money saying: 'Jim's doing the same job as me and I want what he earns';
- never ask for more money because you're broke (managing your finances is your responsibility and not the company's);
- gain trust over a period of time by building up a portfolio of successes and achievements;
- even if you've been promoted once, the second promotion isn't automatic.

> **TIP**
>
> Your abilities with the 3 C's – **c**ommunication, **c**oaching and **c**omputer skills – will mark you out for success. Have some achievements to demonstrate each of them. You don't have to be an expert.

Prepare your case

Keep evidence of all you're doing for the company. You need a ring binder or folder in which to keep letters, memos and reports that support your case. Even if a project wasn't a howling success, it could still have added up to useful research. Keep letters or e-mails you get from satisfied customers.

Now is not the time to:

- enquire about sabbaticals – even if you have been with the company a long time;
- ask for an extended holiday, or for leave without pay;
- ask about working in other areas or branches of the company, or abroad.

Consolidate now

This is the time to consolidate all you've done and give more to your current boss. Handling your appraisal and salary review will be the final stages in your first promotion programme – you'll be building on all you've done. You'll already have **demonstrated** what you can do, and provided the **evidence** of success: now you formally **ask** for entry into the next stage up.

> Useful Web site to rehearse a job appraisal or a talk: *Authentic Speaking* at **www.speakingcircles.com**.

10

KEEPING AHEAD

Congratulations. Your hard work and the long days have paid off. You've got promotion. But is that the end of the story? You've climbed further up the ladder, but is this where you intend to stay? Is this where the striving stops?

Don't be tempted into complacency. Maintain your hard-earned reputation for hard work and reliability. Promotion doesn't entitle you to late starts and early departures, and it would be unwise to cut corners now. You are shouldering a heavier burden and you've got to show you can cope with it. If necessary, put in more hours.

Another risk is that after a while, when you discover that a manager's situation is far from comfortable, you might think you're 'doing too much' and almost resent the company for the burden it's placing on you. This mood has sabotaged many a promising career. Make sure you remind yourself you wanted both the extra work and the extra benefits.

Get back to your secret promotion plan, but don't exhaust yourself physically or mentally. Take adequate vacations and invest in energy 'fixes' such as regular massage or aromatherapy treatments, health club membership and exercise such as walking and swimming.

Don't be too obvious about making moves for your next promotion. Your boss has sorted you out for the time being: let him or her move on to other things. He or she will want to see you concentrating on your new job. Remember the military maxim: secure your conquered ground before moving on to the next campaign.

Motivate others

To keep on top of the new job, you'll need to build on the leadership skills you've demonstrated already. The ability to inspire others is vital if you're ambitious. You can motivate others by:

- Praising good work – the work doesn't have to be excellent.
- Saying 'thanks'. If you're around when people are leaving the office at the end of the day, don't just say 'goodnight' – say 'thanks'. If you know they've done something well that day, refer to it.
- Not just criticizing when someone is doing something wrong. Instead, explain how it should be done.
- Involving people in projects from the earliest possible moment. Say how you want things done, but invite better, alternative ideas. If there are any, use them and give credit where it's due.
- Trying to get pay increases for good people where you can.
- Leading by example to earn respect.

TIP

Once you're promoted, don't be tempted to 'dump' work on juniors. Delegate carefully: still do the core planning and managing, plus extra tasks. If you begin 'dumping', it will soon be noticed and you may not get the next promotion.

Have a help network

You may be someone who puts in large bursts of work and then gets very tired or even exhausted or depressed. Many managers find this happens. Try to build into your life some 'preventive medicine' for this. Try booking regular holidays and breaks in your diary instead of waiting until you're worn out, then finding that everything's booked up or you can't go because other key staff are away too.

If you're a working mum or single dad, you shouldn't be doing a second shift at home: some cash spent on a cleaner, for example, will take some of the chores away.

Get things delivered

There are shopping delivery services in most cities. Even if you don't feel you need a cleaner, you might welcome an ironing service. See home delivery services, ironing services and the rest as your help network. You should certainly have a list of all your local take-always pinned up in your kitchen. You could buy 'awkward items' like towels and sheets mail order. (The White Company simplifies colour co-ordination! orders@thewhitecompany.co.uk) Try all the home shopping catalogues for electrical and kitchen goods. Don't forget you can use the Internet for shopping. The more you can have delivered, the more of your time is your own.

You may even be able to spend a couple of hours on work when the rest of the weekend runs smoothly, maybe by getting up early on a Sunday morning. The more organized your life is, work done at home will seem less like a chore.

Look after yourself

> **TIP**
>
> Staying fit is essential. The higher up you go at work, the more stress there is. Keeping fit is vital. If you really dislike sports, try to walk for an hour a day on Saturday and Sunday – city walking is fine.

It may be very expensive to belong to a local health club and you may not use it enough to justify the cost. Instead, think in terms of the 'day ticket' including use of all facilities at a spa or leisure hotel. Some hotels do a six or ten visit ticket at a cheap rate.

Keep on top

Don't forget that your very strengths can pull you down – people can ruin their success just by becoming too tired.

> **TIP**
>
> When you're promoted, besides the feeling of success there's also a 'pain barrier' – things just don't feel so comfortable as before. Get through the initial discomfort. You will grow into the new role. Don't even think of jacking it in and demoting yourself.

Then it's tempting just to do the 'easy' things you know you can do well rather than tackle more challenging roles.

There's no point in spoiling your success by putting your head down and becoming too hands-on again. Your bosses want you to organize others and originate ideas, not just be a 'worker bee'. Bigger and more significant ideas will be expected from you as you climb higher up the career ladder. Your salary is your company's investment in you. When you feel worn out, try to take a short break, return to work renewed and put more into your new role. Do not – repeat not – return to your old role, the one you had before you were promoted. This is a trap that many people fall into.

As you move on up, there may be benefits in addition to the cash: private health insurance, share options, profit share, your own team, a company car or your own office. But the demands on your skills, talents and time are greater. Stick to all the principles that secured you your first promotion.

Useful Web site: still haven't booked that much needed holiday? Try **www.lastminute.com** for in-the-nick-of-time cheap flights and breaks.

Summary

The more responsible and highly paid the job, the fewer applicants there are – two examples of organizations affected by this are the Army and publishing companies. Both these employers attract many candidates at the lower end of the scale, but few candidates for the highly paid demanding positions. Most employers have trouble finding enough staff of the right calibre for the more important roles. Many employees fear taking on too much responsibility.